METAXA STARS

METAXA STARS

The Evolution of a Greek Spirit
Within Generations

ZIKA METAXA

Mataxa Stars: The Evolution of Greek Spirit
Within Generations by Zika Metaxa

Library of Congress Control Number: 2022915053
ISBN: 978-1-959009-08-5 (Hardcover)
ISBN: 978-1-959009-03-0 (Paperback)
ISBN: 978-1-959009-02-3 (Ebook)

SIMPLY
GOOD PRESS
EST. 2012

Published by Simply Good Press, Montclair, NJ

DEDICATION & ACKNOWLEDGMENTS

This book is dedicated . . .

*To **Angelos** and **Andreas***
***Andreas** and **Angelos** aka "Angy"*
May our Greek spirit reach the next generation
through a passionate but unbiased path and channel.

*To my one and only real shining star **Dimitri***
May I always be the moon, sun and earth for you.
The Universe is not big enough to
shelter my love for you.

May your life be filled with joy,
peace, love, and many stars.
I love you more. The end.
Mom

~Z.M.

THANK YOU TO . . .

*Christine Whitmarsh for all your patience, good
vibes, and humor throughout our journey together.
Thank you for helping me make my dreams come true.
Thank you for knowing exactly what I
meant although it was Greek to you!
Thank you for working with me from the
other side of the world at odd hours.
Thank you for being there for me.*

*Jane Tabachnick for all your guidance,
experience and support.*

*Alexandra Kappatou for all your wisdom, presence,
patience. Thank you for helping me find my own star.*

*Last but not least, thank you Kate Loftus, my Kate,
my Metta, my coach and friend who brought the
stories in this book to the surface to finally be told.*

*Dear reader, this book is in your hands today because
of Kate's magical wand opening the doors of my soul!*

TABLE OF CONTENTS

My great-grandmother Despina and her children

INTRODUCTION

Meet the Metaxas

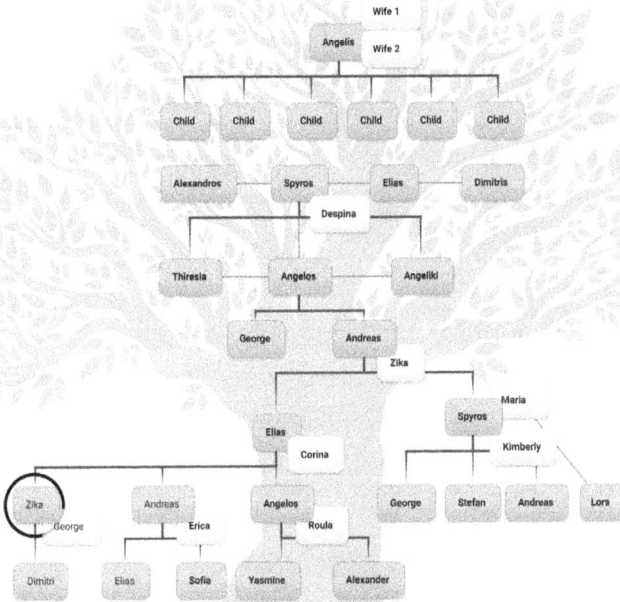

Angelis — Wife 1 / Wife 2

Child — Child — Child — Child — Child — Child

Alexandros — Spyros — Elias — Dimitris

Despina

Thiresia — Angelos — Angeliki

George — Andreas

Zika

Elias — Corina

Spyros — Maria

Kimberly

Zika — George | Andreas — Erica | Angelos — Roula | George | Stefan | Andreas | Lora

Dimitri | Elias | Sofia | Yasmine | Alexander

Flaming Vodka Shots

At one time in my marketing career, I was the brand manager at a multinational company representing an umbrella of various liquors and spirits. One of the products I represented was Smirnoff vodka.

For one particular meeting at Smirnoff promotions, I had in mind a "budget on fire" theme. Flaming shots were trendy in bars at the time so my idea was to make and present a flaming shot with vodka at the meeting. I had queried many bartenders before but no one had such a recipe so I had to get resourceful. As you are about to read in this book, being resourceful is in my blood!

I thought of adding a few drops of clear alcohol in the vodka shots, and indeed I produced a stunning flaming shot! The only two minor problems were that once the meeting was over and I had shooed everyone out of the conference room: a) I had to persuade the people attending the meeting to NOT drink the pure alcohol spiked shots, and b) I had to figure out a way to put out the flaming shots. I blew and blew but the flames did not burn out. Quite the opposite!

I watched as the flames grew bigger and higher, and worried that my brilliant idea was going to cost us the client account and worse, end up burning down a conference room and maybe the whole building if we didn't watch out. Finally, to my great relief, I was able to extinguish the flames, rinse the shots down a drain so nobody would accidentally drink them, and breathe a big sigh of relief.

There were many other stories from my time working in marketing at the multinational corporation too. Every liquor seemed to have its own entertaining tale!

The Famous Metaxas

Speaking of entertaining tales—welcome to the story of my family! I am a genuine Greek woman with a true love for my country, family, Greek origins, and—more than anything in the world—my only son, Dimitris. He is the star and sunshine of my life. I also love animals, which is why we currently have four dogs, a bird, and a bearded dragon! I love reading and writing, and I am already the author of a children's book. With this book you are now reading, I have challenged myself to share the story of my Greek family in English, my second language.

Why? Because I feel that we all have issues with our families occasionally or constantly. I am no family counselor or professional therapist. I am sharing my own experiences and thoughts as if I were chatting with friends over coffee or, even better, a famous Metaxa beverage. Empathy can go a long way, especially when it comes to family.

Who is my family?

Around Greece, there are billboards with one simple word in black and yellow: METAXA. That's my family's name. My name is Zika Metaxa, and my family produces the famous Metaxa.

Metaxa is a word familiar to most Greeks, especially those who have ever attended soccer games in giant stadiums, where our ever-present billboards resided prominently behind the nets. This was true over the twenty years between the 1970s through the '90s, especially for international, televised matches year-round. In the 1970s especially, watching sports on TV was novel and exciting, so people were even more impressed to see the Metaxa ads!

3

This word *Metaxa* created discussions among those who saw the billboard and, as the television signals broadcasted the images around the world, made every Greek watching the match proud.

I wrote this book to tell the behind-the-scenes story of that single word on those billboards—Metaxa. I wrote it to honor my ancestors, who managed the unimaginable over a century ago. They managed to create, produce, and distribute brandy in Greece, of all places. Brandy is much more common in European countries like France. In fact, before Metaxa came along, the idea of making brandy in Greece was as unusual as producing sake (native to Japan) in Norway!

It all started in 1888 with a few bottles my great-grandfather Spyro produced in an old, abandoned distillery. Metaxa then grew to tens of thousands of cases shipped from Greece worldwide to duty-free shops, hotels, restaurants, bars, clubs, houses, everywhere. We had local and international TV advertisements, billboards in the Mundial Basket in Spain (a popular basketball game played every four years), as well as a strong visual presence at the international soccer games I mentioned earlier.

There are many Metaxa stories, from my great-grandfather to my grandfather, father, uncle, and finally to myself and my role in the family business, even after it was sold to a multinational corporation in 1989.

Personal, emotional, and funny stories and lessons can be found in the heart of any family, especially when that family is in business together, sharing more time than a typical family unit—a *lot* more time! I wrote this book to share those stories and lessons of my ancestors who started this business in 1888 to modern times, including my own experiences working in the family business.

The story of Metaxa is a real story in which generations go through turmoil, overcome challenges, and bond in the process. In a family business, while you're learning from the previous generations' mistakes, you're also constantly carving out space for the next generations to find their voices and learn all new lessons. In a family business, the future will erase the past and create a solid present.

There is a place for you, the reader, in this book too. Even if you're not a Metaxa, you will be an honorary branch on our family tree in these pages. Hopefully you will laugh and learn with us and, most importantly, find the value, wisdom, and humor in *your* family tree!

Just as family businesses have their challenges, so do families who are not in business together. All families have their good moments, bad moments, and what some younger family members might see as their embarrassing moments. I'm taking you behind the scenes of all those Metaxa moments to show you that no matter what you think of your family, there are lessons to be learned, even in the chapters you'd rather ignore.

Even when the flames threaten to get out of control and hit the ceiling (this will make sense when you get to the Zika chapter of the family business!), there is always something to be learned! Welcome to my family story.

PART I

Persevere

CHAPTER 1

Distilling a Dream

It is a Greek tradition to name children after their fathers' parents.

Therefore, the Metaxa family story is filled with familiar names—from Spyros and Elias Metaxa, my great-grandfather and great-granduncle, to Elias and Spyros Metaxa, my father and uncle, to my grandmother and namesake, Zika. My brothers Andreas and Angelos were named after my grandfather Andreas and his brother Angelos. My brother's son Elias was named after our father. My uncle Spyros named his sons Andreas and George after their grandfathers. The same goes for most Greek families. The way that in other parts of the world, a son would be "junior," named after his father, in Greece we simply bestow the names themselves to honor family members from generation to generation.

The story of my family's business begins in 1870 with nine brothers and one sister who became merchants and then brokers. Both of these occupations were extremely difficult then, and they still are today. Being a merchant was the opposite of a "formal job" handed down from one's parents.

It was a daily hustle, going from village to village, networking, listening for conversations about potential opportunities to buy a commodity (like wool, for instance) and then sell it on the spot for a profit. It required thinking on your feet, creativity, and improvisation—qualities that would serve our family well in the future business!

It was in 1888 when two of the nine brothers, Spyros and Elias started gradually incorporating beverages into their merchandising business. This is how the now worldwide known brand, the famous Metaxa started.

It all happened when Spyros Metaxa found an old cheap distillery in one of the buildings he bought. Spyros and his family members were doing all sorts of business those days. Mainly commerce but also real estate although that term had not been invented yet in the 1800s. They were buying and selling buildings and land. Gradually the other brothers became involved and eventually the Metaxa spirit, or cognac as they called it, found its niche position in the Greek market. They used to call it cognac in the early days but were prohibited to do so later on, as cognac is named after the city in France which produces it. It is not at all a Greek origin product—quite the opposite!

This business started for two big reasons which along with other factors led to its success. First, the family was general merchants and brokers, and thus had sources to sustain a new business. Second, early on they started exporting first in nearby countries such as Turkey and then all over Europe. The next generations that took over worked extremely hard and managed to not only maintain this success, but also expanded the business in unimaginable ways. By the 1960's, the third generation, my father Elias and uncle Spyros took the business to another dimension.

Since they were kids, their father Andreas (my grandfather) brought Elias and Spyros daily to the small factory that housed Metaxa at the time.

My grandfather Andreas takes
my father Elias and Uncle Spyros to work

They grew up knowing that this business was their future—and a remarkable future indeed. They started working in the family business in 1956 after they both completed their studies, my father having studied at a winery in Dijon France, while my uncle studied marketing in the U.S.

The brothers Elias and Spyros were an extremely strong and volatile combination, two totally different personalities working together. And as the third generation is usually the stronger one they brought the business to its peak.

After World War II the Metaxas built a new, modern factory where they bottled 3000 bottles daily and started exporting Metaxa spirits and ouzo worldwide, simultaneously creating outstanding advertisements. My father was the master blender constantly excelling the taste and producing various new products, thus increasing the product line. The bottling and packaging were also constantly upgraded. My uncle focused on the marketing and public relations side while also working wonders in those fields. Bottles in hand, they both started traveling all over Greece and then abroad.

In a few years Metaxa became the first selling brandy in the Duty Free Shops (DFS_. Ninety percent of travelers leaving Greece had purchased at least one bottle in the DFS. Over the years and decades, Metaxa became synonymous with Greece and the most wanted gift or souvenir from Greece.

My grandfather Andreas was lucky enough to live until 1980 and watch the evolution of the famous Metaxa with immense pride. He also enjoyed his grandchildren with his wife and my namesake Zika.

My grandfather Andreas   *My grandmother Zika*

After my grandfather's death my grandmother Zika entered the business management and was the second woman after my great grandmother Despina to do so. My grandmother passed away in 2001.

In 1989 Metaxa was sold to DIAGEO multinational company.

CHAPTER 2

Determination Amongst Disruption

Little Elias

When my father Elias was a small boy he and his family lived in a house with a trap door in the living room floor. His father had made it in case they had to hide from the Germans, first during World War II and then afterward, the Greek Civil War (1944-1949).

Little Elias, a small boy with gray green eyes, slightly chubby, and very intelligent would pass most of his days, months, in the house. The Germans were raiding the streets and it was forbidden to go out especially for children and women.

So little Elias sat next to the closed window watching every movement in the street from through the blinds. Their house was situated in the center of town so there was a lot to watch. Elias had to watch carefully though, as there were also bullets that would "visit" their house through the windows.

He watched carefully through the blinds, for hours at a time, with the intensity kids today watch video games.

The violence was the real life version of today's simulated games. It was no virtual reality for the people of this time, It was daily reality. People were shot, small children were terrorized. Little Elias never forgot how a German soldier broke a small boy's arm, just because he was begging for a piece of bread. While Elias was in the house watching everything, my yiayia ("grandmother" in Greek) Zika was very busy.

Zika was a beautiful slender tall woman with black hair, pale skin and gray green eyes just like Elias. She was also very intelligent and had learned a few basic German words and phrases. Risking her life, she would go out almost daily, running and hiding between buildings to avoid bullets, in order to find some basic groceries to feed her family. She paid either in Golden Pounds (lira) or by trading Metaxa spirits for groceries.

The few things she got, she hid under her clothes and ran back home again amidst the spray of bullets in the air around her. As the groceries she procured were usually not enough to feed a family, she created the recipe for this tasty product—the yolk from the egg, sugar, and coffee. She would blend by fork for at least half an hour and use it to nourish her boys.

After the World War ended, the Civil War began with the English helping the Greeks get rid of the communists. English soldiers set up camp on the top floor of the Metaxa home, which had a terrace. They shot the communists on the street from that terrace. This meant more real life action games for little Elias to witness. No wonder when he grew up one of his favorite hobbies was shooting . . . errrr . . . I mean hunting!!

Meanwhile pappou ("grandfather" in Greek) Andreas and his brothers were busy producing bulk brandy. In addition to enjoying it as a beverage, they would also use it as medicine. Because of its multiple uses, and since it was low cost and quite tasty, people would queue outside their store in long lines to buy it. The lines frequently had people pushing and occasionally trying to climb the stairs in order to get some of the amazing nectar.

The Metaxa brothers did not want the Germans to find out the recipe for this tasty brandy. God, the Universe, or plain luck helped their wish come true. Alongside the store which sold the Metaxa in bulk, they also owned warehouses. Both were situated in Piraeus, the main port of Greece.

In the warehouses they had barrels, and in those days there was a bronze tap at the end of the barrel to extract the liquid. This was bad for the product as the bronze ruined its taste. So when a German General raided the warehouse and demanded to obtain the Metaxa recipe, the Metaxas invited him to taste some straight from the tap of the barrel.

He eagerly rushed to do so only to spit it out whilst cursing and telling all the Germans that this brandy was awful, and that the Greeks must be extremely desperate to drink it. Little did he know that by the end of the century, that brandy would be a bestseller in his own country!

The Modern Metaxas

From the ruins of the second World War and then the Civil War, the modern Metaxa factory was built.

The 1940s were extremely arduous for my great grandfather Spyros and his brother Elias. Greece had to collect and rebuild ruins on all levels. The same applied to the Metaxas who had to start from scratch. They had to rebuild the factory and they scraped money together to pay the few employees they had. They could barely afford the everyday necessities for their own households.

In 1945 the Metaxas got a loan from the National Bank of Greece and were able to restore the original distillery that had been damaged in the wars, and buy new machinery.

In 1956 Spyros and Elias took over.

Three traits characterized those years and the future of the family business: resilience in the face of obstacles, persevering through hard work, and innovating based on a vision for the future.

As a result of these constant traits, there were three huge milestones in the Metaxa business during that time.

1. The start up of the factory
2. Exports in the US and Canada as well as Europe
3. In 1954 Angelos Metaxa passed away and so did George Metaxa two years later.

So Elias and Spyros had to come back from their studies and take over.

My father Elias had just finished his winery studies in Dijon but Spyros didn't manage to conclude his studies in Detroit. Their father Andreas was still director of the company and so his sons were working with him

During this time, in the 1950's and 1960's my Uncle Spyros and his brother, my father Elias worked extremely hard. They had to take care of the inheritances as well as update the business. They rebuilt the factory and the warehouses, bought office equipment, and hired workers, employees and distributors. They worked closely with advertising agencies and came up with legendary ads and slogans.

Magazine Ad for Metaxa 1970s

After George's death in 1956 my father bought a small truck and went all over Greece selling Metaxa and setting up distributors in all the provinces and islands. The distributors were natives of the islands or villages who knew all the locals and loved and promoted Metaxa as if it was their own business. Most of them or their children were still working for the company when it was sold. They all had extremely good relationships with the family and I myself remember visiting them often as a kid with my parents and later working with them. Each one of these individuals portrayed their local community and had an outstanding personality.

For example our distributor in Rhodes, Mike, had a unique way of getting everyone to drink Metaxa every day. Mike was a big tall, always happy and loud man. Whenever he went out for dinner, which was almost the very day, he would greet the customers of a restaurant or tavern by declaring loudly, "Happy Birthday!!!" and ordering free Metaxa for all.

Scenes from the Award Winning Movie Zorba the Greek

The publicity efforts worked and the company grew rapidly. By 1960 the distillery had 160 workers and employees, brand new modern equipment, and dynamic advertisements in many countries. The famous Metaxa, emerging from the ruins of two wars and many obstacles, was now producing 10,000 bottles daily.

CHAPTER 3

Making it Work

Resilience . . . Easier said than done!! I can only imagine the resilience that kept my ancestors going before and especially after two wars. I am sure that in both cases it had to do with survival and determination to keep going on no matter what. I'm sure they felt as though they were thrown in the middle of the ocean and had to find and reach land without knowing how to swim.

Then, once the wars were finally over, they were ready for new beginnings!

In the 1960s, when Elias and Spyros were busy distributing Metaxa all over Greece and Europe, they decided to move the old factory from Piraeus (the port) to another area and rebuild a brand new factory .

My father Elias found an incredible location in Kifissia, a suburb of Attica, which is where the factory is still located today. This location was ideal and with some effort, Elias was able to track down the owner. But it took a lot of patience and tons of discussion to persuade him to sell.

Once the owner finally agreed, Elias and Spyros had to then persuade their father Andreas to move the factory to the new location. Andreas refused to go along with this project as he knew they didn't have enough money, and he also knew he personally did not have the stamina to undergo this operation.

Elias, showing the true meaning of resilience, took on the entire operation himself.

Like Hercules in ancient Greek mythology and like a true Superman nowadays, he managed to get a loan which more than covered their needs. He relentlessly proceeded on his own to build the new factory, and move the entire operations and equipment that was in good condition from Piraeus to Kifissia, investing in new modern equipment as well.

Elias worked non stop with a clear vision and determination. His studies in oenology (the study of wines) helped him immensely. The new operations grew quickly and flourished.

Meanwhile, as all of this was happening in Greece, Elias's brother Spyros was extremely busy, traveling abroad selling Metaxa. Wherever he went, he always had a bottle of Metaxa in his bag, networking, promoting, and opening new doors and businesses. He was great at PR and made numerous friends on the road. He also had sneaky creative ways of getting the word out about the product. On airplanes he would always "forget" his duty free shop bag containing Metaxa on purpose knowing that someone would pick it up, usually sneak a taste, and quickly get hooked.

He always had a bag with bottles of Metaxa in his car too. Whenever my uncle went to a restaurant and they didn't have Metaxa on hand,he took it out, had the owner taste it and gave it to him as a gift, but ONLY if the owner promised to display it prominently on his bar.

While traveling to the United States, although he was on an extremely tight budget, he chose to stay at the five star Plaza

Hotel in New York. There, he presented himself as a wealthy and successful entrepreneur from Greece selling brandy and other liquors.

To sell this impression, he rented a limousine and cruised daily from New York to Astoria in Queens, where there were many Greeks as well as many other cultural communities. With his charming, witty personality, good looks and great sense of humor he made numerous friends along the way (and even more numerous girlfriends!). But he was always focused on his goal, to establish the family business by selecting distributors or agents who would sell and represent Metaxa. He worked hard to create a distribution network throughout New York City that would get our spirit into bars, restaurants, hotels—any business that would agree to sell it! This was a huge vision for an unknown small Greek brand, especially then in the sixties.

Spyros and Elias were two totally different characters with distinct personalities. But both men were extremely intelligent and hard working, so together, they were an extremely strong duo in business. Two boys who grew up during and after the second world war and then transitioned as adults into the crazy sixties. They watched their parents struggle to obtain the basics for them and then gradually started and maintained a business during those hard times. Two boys who grew up hiding from the Germans to establish an empire in Germany and almost all over the world.

When my Uncle Spyros later returned and saw the new Metaxa Distilleries that Elias had built, he was left speechless at what his brother had accomplished! Little Elias had turned into a real life Hercules, carrying the weight of his family's business, and legacy, on his strong back.

At the heart of the Metaxa roots were two Greek Gods—Elias as Hercules, known for his great strength, and Spyros as Dionysus, the god of wine and ecstasy.

Two different lives, two different paths, but one common background and vision, to make Metaxa work—no matter what.

A Metaxa Family Portrait: Corina

Beautiful Sad

My mother Corina was and still is a rare beauty inside and outside.

Corina the sad bride who tried so hard, even in the face of rejection by her future mother-in-laws, and eventually managed to persevere and become a happy wife and mother.

Corina and her twin sister Amalia were brought up by their father Vassilis. Pappou Vassilis was a one-of-a-kind human being—businessman, teacher, great philosopher. He was a doting, attentive father who brought up his daughters single handedly with dignity, love and a lot of patience. This could not have been easy for a tall elegant handsome man in his early forties, and during and after a war. It is not easy for any parent to take care of two identical, spirited, beautiful twin girls.

Vassilis patiently guided them through life, constantly there for them as a great teacher and parent in all ways. Later on he was always there for me as my godfather, guiding me with valuable lessons about life. I was lucky to get to know him well before he passed away when I was eighteen. It's no wonder Corina and Amalia absolutely adored him.

One can easily understand the pain Corina went through as a young bride when, on the day every girl dreams of going to the church on her father's arm, she was accompanied by an almost stranger, her godfather.

This pain or rejection accompanied Corina all her life. Her life was a turmoil of ups and downs. She had a difficult relationship with her in-laws and her peers. But over the years, immersed in Elias's constant love, with her own natural resilience and personal grit, she managed to find balance and a happy life.

Balance

Balance. It sounds simple but it is one of the most difficult things in life. Balance requires a lot of work, everyday work, especially in a marriage.

Corina initially as a young bride found it difficult to obtain balance in her life and relationships. She was pregnant with me months after her wedding and had to face a very difficult mother-in-law, and simultaneously manage responsibilities as a mother, a wife, and a member of a highly visible, public-facing family business.

The death of her beloved father was a huge milestone in my mother's life. He was her rock and the one she would run to every day for solace. He advised her on everything, especially issues with her mother-in-law and her three children (after me she gave birth to Andreas and Angelos). His advice was gold—always wise and dignified.

When her father passed away, Corina was totally lost.

She had to pick up her life from the emotional ruins and start from scratch, like picking up pebbles on the beach one by one and building her own castle. She had to create her own sense of balance in a difficult world.

So, Corina covered her fears and insecurities with a no-worries mask. She became an expert at pushing her inner feelings deep down, making sure that they would not resurface. She got a Masters Degree in "How to not talk about your feelings."

This was a legacy which she passed on to her children. They, in turn, had to learn and excel in a totally opposite themed Masters Degree.

The degree my brothers and I earned was one that required digging deep into self awareness, uncovering inherited beliefs, and filtering them for new realities in a new world where feeling emotions was no longer discouraged. Our life degree was about carving our own paths based on experiences and inner knowledge. Our degree was earned through stumbling, climbing mountains, and crying many tears while banging our heads against all the walls built to keep us in "the old ways" and prevent us from forging new pathways. Our degree eventually led to balance, but only after we studied hard and broke the chains that bound us.

It was the inner struggles and soul searching that bred into my brothers and I, the resilience and patience that opened the door to balance and freedom.

PART II

Savour

CHAPTER 4

My Crazy Lazy Eye

(A Story of Perseverance!)

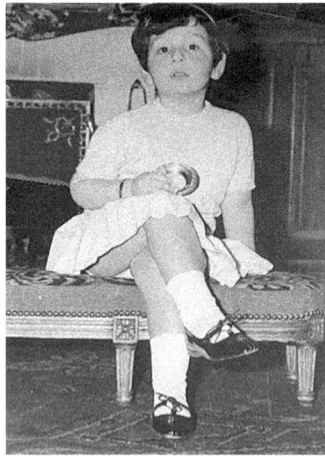

Me as a child

Life forms identical patterns. These patterns are much more than similar or purely coincidental paths in the lives of families, generation after generation. In my family, it's not only names repeating themselves, but real life stories repeated over and over, again and again.

Just like her mother-in-law Zika, my mother Corina was a sad rejected bride. Later, I would repeat the same story on my own.

Just like her mother-in-law Zika had experienced giving birth to my Uncle Spyros, Corina experienced a difficult childbirth. My grandmother Zika gave birth to a son who would ultimately be scarred down the middle of his body from a life saving surgery (for more on this story please see "A Metaxa Family Portrait: My Grandmother Zika" later in this book). My mother Corina gave birth to me, like Spyros, also scarred and branded for life.

Corina had a difficult childbirth. She struggled for hour after hour, begging her obstetrician for a caesarian, but he was adamant that she should have a natural childbirth. She glared with frustration at this stranger who had only been her doctor since her seventh month of pregnancy. She had replaced her original doctor when her friends raved about this one—this man who was now insisting that she deliver me naturally, even though nature was in strong disagreement that this was the best plan.

In those days they used forceps to deliver hesitant babies like me. As the doctor struggled to deliver me with forceps, ignoring Corina's desperate pleas for a c-section, one of the forceps hit me in the face—brutally.

Newborn babies are like playdough, the slightest less-than-gentle touch, can leave a mark. I was molded by iron. Being yanked out of my mother by steel pliers left the right side of my face bruised and my right eye swollen shut.

What a grand, albeit shocking entrance I made to this world—Zika has arrived, everyone take notice!

Corina was inconsolable. Her baby, her first child, a child born of love . . . looking like a war victim. She couldn't stop crying, even as the doctor matter of factly informed her that "it was nothing, it would pass in a few days."

Just like her mother-in-law Zika, Corina at childbirth was left holding a traumatized, scared, traumatized newborn. And just like her mother-in-law, she consented to the Greek traditions and wishes of the inlaws and named her beautiful but scared daughter—Zika.

My Grandma Zika

It took many decades for my grandmother Zika to finally accept my mother Corina as family and establish a healthy relationship with her. Many decades with ups and downs (more downs than ups).

What made this relationship even more difficult was the fact that we all lived in the same building. A beautiful building in the best area of Athens facing the palace where the Kings used to live. The building had six floors. The first, second, and third floor were rented to our neighbors. On the fourth floor lived Elias, Corina, and my brothers and I. On the fifth floor lived my uncle Spyros and on the sixth floor Andreas and my grandmother Zika.

This meant constant parades up and down flights of stairs, and sometimes by elevator, of noisy children, and nannies, as well as kids' parties, adult parties—and a family dog! In the midst of all the turmoil and lack of privacy, there lived a bride and her mother-in-law, stuck in the walls of their tense relationship.

Zika was not the most discreet mother-in-law either! She was a human security camera, always checking who was coming and going and the reason for their comings and goings. If she heard me or my brothers crying, there was no polite phone call to check if everything was okay—she would barge right through our front door to check for herself.

Of course there were the good times too, our typically loud Greek family lunches and gatherings. And fortunately, despite her rocky relationship with my mother, my grandma Zika always had a soft spot for me. The feeling was mutual too. Each day, I would run up the flights of stairs in the building to visit with her. One of my favorite parts is how she would open her huge wardrobe and let me try on her fancy dresses. Some of my favorites in her collection were the fancy 1920's "Charleston style" flapper dresses. I could just look at those and feel the fun she must have had while wearing them!

Later, when I was older, she would give me beautiful clothes she had bought but never worn. She called her home "The Boutique."

When I was in my late teens and I would go up to visit for a cup of tea, she would always serve me whisky instead. In her opinion, tea was only for sick people! To this day I think I must have inherited her opinion and acquired her taste for whiskey.

My Crazy, Lazy Eye

After my literally breathtaking entrance to this world I gradually evolved from a cute little girl trying on her grandma's dresses, to an eventual little ninja, and later on, to the queen of an inferiority complex. It all began with my crazy, lazy eye, damaged at birth by the steel forceps.

My parents found the best eye doctor in Europe, based in Dusseldorf Germany. When I was three years old I underwent my first major eye surgery. The outcome was good. At least my right eye, which was partially closed until then, was now open. Although it was not as open as the left one, and had a bit of a droop.

For years at school, it seemed like my classmates were either constantly quizzing me about my crazy eye, or making fun of it. The eye doctor in Dusseldorf treated my crazy, lazy eye for years. My grandma Zika accompanied us to the visits regularly, chatting with the doctor in fluent German. When I was fifteen years old, my eye doctor recommended another doctor in Munich for my next surgery. So off we went to Munich without a second thought, and with high expectations for a perfect result. I couldn't wait to go back to school with two normal eyes—no more teasing!

On the day of the operation I woke up with chicken pox. Ugh! I must have caught it from my brother Angelos who had it just before we left for Germany. Nevertheless, the medical team at the hospital in Munich sanitized the whole surgery room, and the doctor proceeded with the operation.

I woke up with a black mask on *both* eyes which I had to wear all day every day for five days. I went from one crazy, lazy eye, to being under a shroud of total darkness, unable to see out of either eye. And as if this were not enough I also got my period for the first time on that day! I remember vividly those long days and nights lying in the room, unable to see anything at all, unable to attend to my daily needs. To this day, I have so much empathy and respect for blind people.

I patiently underwent all the long blind days in Germany, dreaming of the happy ending the doctors had promised me and my family. These days were a great introduction to the art of resilience which would become a theme in my life.

After the five days of darkness the doctor gave me a black "pirate patch" to wear on my operated eye. Let there be light again—partially! At least then I could go out for lunch with my parents, doing my best to ignore the weird glances at my pirate patch. I kept reassuring myself—when I leave Germany, my eyes will be the same, normal for the first time. "No more crazy lazy eye. Finally a normal Zika." This mantra gave me the strength and patience required to get through.

On the day that they were finally going to remove my ugly pirate patch and I could leave the clinic in Germany forever, I was so excited I could hardly sleep. Then, when the time came, my parents sat at my bedside while I lay patiently and the doctor removed the stitches from my eye.

I could hardly breathe. I could feel everything but was oblivious to the pain. All I wanted was to see my face in the mirror.

And then . . . I did.

It was exactly the same as before the surgery! No difference at all. Nada. I wanted to cry and yell and scream and hit the mirror all at the same time! Why had I gone through all this? What was the point???

The doctor, showing no emotion (which made me even angrier), said he was sorry, he had done everything possible. My parents were also devastated by the results. But there was nothing left to do except leave the clinic and return home to Greece.

Perseverance

Back at home, I had to pick up my emotional ruins and return to school and face more of the dreaded bullying. Of course none of my classmates noticed anything different about my eye since the German doctor had not been able to fix it. The bullies picked up exactly where they left off, teasing me about my crazy eye.

Meanwhile, as soon as we were back, my perseverant, resilient father Elias started researching and corresponding with doctors all over the world who could undertake my case. He refused to quit until he found someone.

One day in 1980 someone recommended the famous plastic surgeon Dr. Ivo Pitanguy in Rio de Janeiro. Pitanguy was a legend. People from all over the world traveled to Brazil to his famous private clinic to undergo plastic surgery, especially women of course. He was the king of reconstructive surgery. Although he had a very elite clientele, he frequently operated for free on people in need, for example kids who had been seriously burned in accidents.

My family was determined to get Dr. Pitanguy to accept me as a patient. But in 1980 communication was not as simple as it is today. There were no mobile phones or email.

So in genuine perseverant Metaxa Spirit, my father Elias managed not only to contact Dr. Pitanguy via handwritten letters and Telex (a kind of modern telegraph similar to today's fax machines), but also to get us a meeting with him. It was Christmas when we met at his beautiful chalet in Gstaad Switzerland.

The doctor was a short man with a taller than life personality and charm. With a deep voice, clever witty eyes, an engaging smile, and jet black hair he had his own aura about him. No wonder his nickname was the magician. Each day, using his short but strong arms and hands, Dr. Pitanguy performed miracles, transforming people's lives with his magic surgical wands.

After examining me, the doctor said that not only could he reconstruct my eye, he could also fix the deviated septum in my nose that had caused me breathing problems my whole life. Two for one—lucky Zika!

I truly believed that Dr. Pitanguy would help me. In addition to being charming, my new doctor was totally sincere (unlike the German doctor). He was honest that the eye result would not be perfect, but it would definitely be much better than it was.

A few months later, along with my parents and my brothers Andreas and Angelos, I packed my bags and traveled from Greece to Brazil for my surgery. It was an unforgettable trip for each of us for various reasons. First there was my upcoming, long awaited operation. Second, now eighteen years old I was being given the opportunity to fly halfway around the world and visit Rio de Janeiro and Sao Paolo! I still remember how shocked I was after we arrived and were driving through the cities, by the non-existent middle class in Brazil—tiny shacks, usually with no running water, sitting next to towering ultra luxurious hotels. The class lines were dramatic and visible. Only the very rich had enough money to go to clubs, celebrate as part of the legendary Carnivale celebrations. It struck me that to simply participate in their own nation's culture, people needed to have enough money to pay the cost of entry. I felt grateful in those moments for my own Greek culture and the privilege I had to experience it.

The next day I was admitted to the Pitanguy clinic, in a comfortable room where I stayed for four days. The day of my surgery, Dr. Pitanguy was waiting for me in the operating room with classical music playing full blast. Between the soothing sounds of musical instruments and of course the anesthesia, I fell instantly asleep and later woke up in my cozy clinic room.

This surgery was much smoother than the first one in Germany. There were no pirate patches afterward, just small stitches and a cast on my nose. But, unlike last time when I felt like an outcast in public, here I blended in. It was very normal for people to parade around in Rio with casts or bruises on their faces, as so many from around the world went there to have plastic surgery, especially by Dr. Pitanguy.

True to his promise, my eye was much better though not perfect. He said he had done all he could, especially with the tightness of my young skin. The surgery on my nose, however, had gone perfectly—I could breathe normally for the first time!

We stayed in Brazil for a total of two weeks, so after my surgery we had the chance to bond as a family, visiting all the tourist attractions both in Rio and Sao Paolo. When it was finally time to leave, I was feeling much more optimistic about my life back in Greece. I was also looking forward to returning to see my first boyfriend Andreas.

My Brother Andreas

But the first Andreas in my life, would always be my brother.

After my grand entrance to this world and a year after my first surgery in Germany, my mother Corina gave birth to my brother Andreas, her second child and first son. The first Metaxa grandson. Although I was only four years old, I still remember the big celebration the Metaxa family held when Andreas was born.

"It's a boy!!"

And what a boy Andreas was! He had blonde hair, white porcelain skin, Maldives turquoise eyes, and red cheeks so adorably chubby that you wanted to take a bite out of them. When we went to the park near our house, people would stop us to get a closer look at the beautiful little baby boy in the royal pram. Those who laid eyes on my brother unanimously agreed—he was the most beautiful baby in the whole world! (Of course most of those eyes were Metaxa eyes, so we were admittedly biased.) Andreas was the baby version of his grandfather of the same name.

Painting of me and my brothers
Angelos and Andreas

The fourth generation of Metaxas had officially arrived. This is a major event for a Greek family. The first grandson and son of the generation. What a joy the birth of my brother was for the whole family including the grandparents—especially the "son" part.

In contrast, after my difficult birth and all the ordeal my mother went through, my father thought he was consoling her when he told her, "Do not worry Corina, the lady in the room next door also had a girl!" Ah, tradition!

This tradition is so important in Greek culture that in several villages and islands, when a man with two sons and two daughters is asked how many children he has, he will say he has two children, and two daughters.

In Greece, people give extreme importance to the sex of the newborn. When a boy is born it is a major celebration. Our tradition states that first born children (and occasionally all children) are named after their paternal grandparents. But if it is a boy AND named after his grandfather, that means a double celebration! This is due to the fact that in Greece most family owned businesses have the family name, the surname, or both. It is assumed that the son will continue the business that shares his name.

So my brother Andreas was named after our grandfather Andreas Metaxa. And when my beautiful brother Andreas many years later had his own son, he was named Elias after my father Elias Metaxa.

For my part, I was thrilled to have a baby brother to cuddle and play with!

My relationship with Andreas was all nice and lovely until when he was around 10 years old, he gave away all my cherished Barbie dolls without asking me.

I was so MAD!

He apparently assumed I was old enough not to play with dolls anymore, so he gave them away to a friend of his. His decision hurt even more because back in those years we didn't have Barbie dolls in Greece. But I had an exceptionally large collection of Barbie dolls thanks to my mother. Whenever she was in Switzerland, she would buy a Barbie from my favorite toy shop there, and bring it home. My collection was precious to me, so I was devastated when Andreas gave it away.

Over the years though, as is common in sibling relationships, Andreas and I moved past the Barbie doll drama and became friends. Today he is an amazing father and husband, and also an impressively creative person with many talents and exquisite taste.

My Complex

Meanwhile, once back in Greece after my (finally) successful eye surgery in Brazil, it wasn't as easy as I thought it would be to move forward with my new "normal life." The past clung to me like an invisible pirate patch over my face. For so many years, I was bullied so much at school that the mantra I created in Germany after the first (failed) surgery—"No more crazy lazy eye. Finally a normal Zika."—grew bigger and bigger in my mind. Finally being normal was all I could think about. For my whole life, I thought that everyone I met only saw my crazy, lazy eye. They thought I was ugly. They didn't see the normal girl with all the personality traits behind it.

These thoughts became the root of a lifelong complex for me. I grew up believing that my damaged eye characterized me. It was my identity. It overwhelmed me and, in my mind, put a black mark over my entire life. Even for years after my eye was fixed, I did not dare look people in the eye, especially boys and later men!

Complexes are trees with roots that are watered and grown by other people.

We are not born with complexes.We acquire them, we take good care of them and they grow. We live with them, they become a part of us. We feel judged, criticized, evaluated, and acknowledged by them. Little hints, casual remarks, and curious looks unveil them.

We try to hide them but they are still there. We try to ignore them but they keep knocking on our door. Knock knock who's there? Knocking and growing.

And then they become larger than life. It feels like they are going to strangle us. They possess us and we possess them.

It takes a lot of inner hard work to accept and remove the pain others have implanted in us. We have to learn to love ourselves—such a cliché but so true. Only by loving and embracing ourselves with positivity will we win the complex war. The war of our inner self with our outer self. The war of insecurity versus self confidence. These two are bigtime enemies!

This war takes years of soul searching and acceptance. I think I have been fighting this war all my life not only with my crazy lazy eye but with certain other parts of my body which I also grew to hate.

This is where my friend PERSEVERANCE appears to save the day. Perseverance is my buddy, my weapon in this war, my ally. I sometimes forget to call in my buddy, and immediately her enemy insecurity swoops in like an evil villain. It is an epic battle, a lifetime struggle. But in the end, with the proper weapons and endless battles, perseverance wins this war.

We are still fighting every day, but fortunately, my friend perseverance and I believe in happy endings.

My Forever Friend (Crazy Lazy Eye, Act II)

My forever friend perseverance was next to me, holding my hand, when I had a *fourth* operation on my eye. This was fourteen years after Dr Pitanguy's surgery in Brazil. I was now a grown woman, thirty years old. My parents and I decided that we could try another surgery since my skin was not so tight anymore and the results would likely be better—maybe even near perfect. Even in the face of this probable improvement, I was still holding tight onto all my complexes.

Again, my father undertook all the correspondence and contact with the doctors. This time we ended up in New York New York! What a grand tour we had, of all the surgery rooms and hospitals. It was a lucky coincidence that my brother Angelos happened to be working in New York at the time too.

So, my mother and I packed and traveled to New York, where I had my fourth surgery at the Eye and Ear Hospital where I stayed for four days. Then I moved into Angelos' apartment and happily caught up with him since I hadn't seen him in a while. My mother and I remained in New York for about two weeks.

This time I had a speedy recovery—and also a speedy realization that once again, perfection had escaped me. The result of the operation was a tad better, but still no two identical eyes.

Was another operation in store for me?

I thought about it and talked it over with my family, but ultimately decided, after all I had gone through—no more surgeries for me thank you!

I was done, emotionally and physically, and so were my parents. I had to roll up my sleeves and enter the battlefield with all my complexes once again.

Sometimes I believe I am still in the ring punching myself . . .

CHAPTER 5

Growing Up Metaxa

Greek Royalty

In the 1960's, royalty still existed in Greece. There were a few well-known families who were considered society's "elite," usually businessmen and their families.These "royal" families mostly had English nannies for their children, a rare privilege since English was not taught in our schools.

We were amongst those lucky ones. King Constantine and his wife Queen Anna Maria used to have parties at the palace, and frequently my parents were among the invited guests. I vividly remember my beautiful mother getting ready to attend those parties, teasing her hair into an elegant hairdo, and slipping on a glamorous gown. SHE was the princess in my eyes!

Even better, was that our house actually faced the palace. After my parents were whisked away to the party, I would run up the stairs to our balcony on the fourth floor. From there I could see the palace with its beautiful gardens.

The gardens were also where my nanny Vicky (whom I adored) would frequently take me over to play with Princess

Alexia. Each day, the English nannies took the children to the National Park next to the palace. There was a nice playground there where the older children would play while the nannies sat on benches pushing the prams carrying the babies. Rather than playing with the other children, I preferred sitting with the nannies, pushing my little pram with my doll in it. From an early age I dreamt of the day when my doll would be replaced by a real baby—I couldn't wait to be a mom!

Then came the 1970's and the King and his family were exiled. Almost overnight, there was no more royalty in Greece. For the elite families, this meant no more palace events. But the people celebrated this transition, as most were against the monarchy.

Meanwhile, in our household, there was great cause for a different type of celebration as my mother gave birth to her second son and third child Angelos, named after my grandfather's brother Angelos. The name suited him perfectly though, as he is a true angel in all senses. My brothers and I were each born about four years apart, so I was seven years older than baby Angelos. Tata! Our roles were clearly defined. Andreas was my best friend and playmate, and Angelos was "my" baby. There is a photo of me at seven years old, giving a bottle to Angelos.

In Greece and around the world, life followed its usual patterns and so did our family—nannies, nurseries, schools, universities, first and last loves, friends, pets, grandparents, uncles and aunties, dramas, and joys.

Elias and Corina were the stars of these multiple Metaxa movies and plot lines. Hard work, perseverance, patience, love and fate, were the directors. And at first, my brother Andreas,

Angelos and I were actors in someone else's story. But in the end, we became directors of our own.

The Factory

The Metaxa Distilleries Factory, founded and constructed by my father Elias, holds many memories for me in its arms. When my brothers and I were young, my father would take us to the factory on Sundays as a little excursion. It was almost an hour drive from our house.

In the garden of the Distillery there was a huge tree, and my father had made a swing which hung from the tree, much to my and my brothers' delight. We spent hours playing there and going for walks in the gardens inside the distilleries. There was a huge garden and a separate area with dogs and chicken.

As the years went by, Spyros and Elias stayed busy expanding the business. But in true Greek tradition, my grandmother put her own stamp on the distillery. She took over two of the offices and transformed them into a kitchen and a dining room. Initially everyone thought this was ridiculous. But we "Zika Metaxas" have our own personality—when we set our mind on something, there is no going back.

The little kitchen took its own place in the distillery where my grandfather Andreas, his wife Zika, and their sons Spyros and Elias would gather for lunch every day. My grandmother made sure that no matter how busy they were, they stopped their work and had lunch together. Gradually these lunches became longer and everyone excitedly anticipated the tasty long Greek lunch break.

Several years later, when my grandfather had passed away, this tradition continued. Whoever was at the office would have lunch even if it was just my uncle or my father. My grandmother Zika was there every day too, and so was I often after school. Years later my uncle and father would entertain their business associates, friends, and politicians in THE dining room.

THE Dining Room

Our family dining room became THE dining room and played a different but major role in our life and business. Infinite discussions have taken place there—business deals, important calls, PR lunches, lonely lunches, and loud, crowded lunches. But every discussion in the dining room was heart to heart, face to face discussions that sealed our lives.

The discussion sometimes involved my grandmother, her husband, sometimes the two brothers, and Uncle Spyros, sometimes my grandmother distilling in me the secrets of life, sometimes my father and I, and other times, a single family member in a private telephone call. No matter what the combination of Metaxas at the table, secrets were spilled, advice was given, plans were made, and in some cases, there were fights that required separate make-up discussions—all in THE dining room. It became our retreat, our time to catch up, to relax—our own Metaxa routine.

Business also seeped into the family dining room, with tastings taking place at the bar with the impressive high stools. My grandfather's, father's, and uncles' offices were in a row one next to the other, all adjourning and leading to the dining room.

The dining room became a token of our family tradition and proof that the distillery was indeed our second home.

★ ★ ★

CHAPTER 6

Fruits of a Family

Elias & Corina
my father and mother

Elias my father

Acceptance Equals Unconditional Love

Mom, mother, mama . . . whatever you call your own. What is the deeper meaning behind the existence of a mother? What is a mother's role on this earth?

"To nurture and take care of her children, of course!"

"To raise her children and set them free into the world, silly!"

"What a ridiculous question, it is to provide for her children, to be a role model, to be a this, to be a that, to be all the things we need her to be . . ."

The true role of a mother has been endlessly speculated on, debated, analyzed and reanalyzed—often on the therapy couch. Throughout history, children of all ages have yearned, pleaded, and fought for approval, acceptance, and unconditional love from their own mothers. Some got their wish and got what they were looking for. But some were left behind with bitter hearts and a lifetime of questions.

When individual family plotlines, dramas, and individual circumstances are stripped away, one thing becomes clear in the relationship between mothers and children: Acceptance Equals Unconditional Love.

To love with every bit of your soul. To accept and cherish wholeheartedly. To be blind to imperfections. To emphasize— to try to understand with your whole soul.

To complete but not compete.

May all mothers, all parents try their best to live up to these expectations, on their unique trip on earth. Maybe then, through the force of their efforts, all future mothers and children, together, will be able to break the chains of the past and set future generations free.

The Fruits of Unconditional Love

What is unconditional love? Is it the name of a song, or a love story, book, or a romantic movie? Perhaps it is perfect little gatherings at home, or big dinner parties at restaurants. Or maybe it is attending friends' weddings or christenings of their children. Or is it year round Valentine Day?

It is all of the above and much more.

Unconditional love was the love of Andreas and Zika. The love of Elias and Corina The love of Zika (me) and George (my ex-husband). The love of my brother Angelos and his wife Roula. The love of my brother Andreas and his wife Erica. And the couple at the heart of our family from the beginning—the love and commitment of Despina and Spyros that built our family.

Unconditional love is more than the heart of those pure love stories. It's also the layers that surround them—the big red hearts, chocolates, flowers, beautiful houses with gardens, happy families, children, perfect (and imperfect) dinner parties, eating out, celebrations, christenings, anniversaries, and birthdays.

It's Christmases and New Years' Eves, year round Valentine's Day, happy travels around the world, a spouse coming home from work every day announcing "honey I'm home." It's cuddles, kisses, promises, gifts, tables full of delicious foods, surprises, laughter, and making love. It's spending season after season together.

Unconditional love is a constant flow of genuine feelings for the other person. It's when you keep thinking of them and how you can make their day and life better, easier. It's when your priorities come second. It's when you really truly want to please the other person no matter what.

It's when you make little surprises out of nothing and give every day a new meaning. It's when you highlight your daily chores with humor. It's when you cannot have enough of each other no matter how many years have gone by. It's missing them constantly, even when they're right in front of you.

It's when your two lives come together into one single life painting, but not on the wall, in your hearts. It's when you feel you can actually move mountains to make your dreams come true, nothing and no one can stop you. It's when you are blind and deaf to problems because your brain and heart are high on adrenaline and serotonin hormones.

It's when you feel like you've run a marathon whether you are excited or exhausted. It's when you forget all the rules you were taught as a kid—you make your own rules. You live by your own standards and norms.

You carve your common paths based on similar beliefs and desires. You don't want to share each other with others. You make new common friends and filter your previous ones. Memories and souvenirs have a special place not only in your house but mostly in your heart. Years are marked by events together. You recall dates and milestones in your life as before and after the event.

Their happiness is your happiness, their worries are yours. Your hearts emphasize with each other. You grow patience with each other. You can read their eyes better than you do books. One look is a full sentence! You can also read their body posture. Certain poses are entire movies. You scan them and instantly know what happened. You become a medium, a fortune teller.

You want to be together but also let the other be free. To love not to obsess or possess. It's to hold in your arms and thoughts, not in an emotional prison. It's to carry not only their children, but also their burdens.

Unconditional love is to always be there, to compromise, to manage your own fears and anger, to try and keep a balance when life is unpredictable and harsh. It's to know how to support yourself with words and actions.

It's to think fast and calmly, to make scenarios that can be easily broken, to erase negativity and replace it with positivity. It's to be okay with your own bad days—to be okay in general.

Unconditional love is to get up and keep going, no matter how many times you fall. It's to keep smiling because you have a constant reason to do so. It's to keep warming each other's hearts.

And when things become hard, because we all have those periods in our lives, unconditional love is to be there. Silent or noisy, calm or busy, present or absent—always there.

Unconditional love is to take insecurities and transform them into securities. It's to caress with words as well as with hands. It's to attend to needs, to nurture.

Unconditional love is to love—no matter what. Unconditional love is a fruit of a relationship, and the fruit of being part of a family.

Elias and Corina

Elias met Corina in 1960—it was fate that brought them together. 24 year old Elias and his buddy Mario met stunning twins Corina and Amalia at a party and asked them out.

On the day of the date Elias, passionate about cars, drove up to the twins' house in his fancy 4 seater sports car. Elias and his friend Mario had decided that Mario would date Corina and Elias, Amalia. But the twin girls, always fighting and teasing each other, argued about who would get to sit next to the driver, Elias. Corina decided it by pushing her twin sister Amalia into the back seat and took her place next to

Elias, where she still sits 61 years later. That night, a love story began that would have many similarities to the love story of Elias's own parents, Andreas and Zika, with similarities seen throughout the Metaxa family tree throughout the generations.

Following that double date, Elias and Corina soon fell hopelessly in love and Elias proposed. Corina accepted on one condition—Elias had to stop car racing. Head over heels in love, he reluctantly agreed.

One obstacle to the love affair was Elias's mother Zika, who would not agree to this marriage, as she was always trying to arrange a marriage for him based on her criteria and not his. As you will learn later in her Metaxa Family Portrait, my grandmother Zika had experienced nearly this exact story with her husband, my grandfather Andrea.

One would think that having gone through a similar story herself, Zika would welcome any wife for her sons. But unfortunately none were good enough. (And what a coincidence the same situation would happen to me later in life!)

So Elias, in true Metaxa spirit, proceeded to put an announcement of his upcoming marriage to Corina in the newspaper.

Zika read the announcement and fainted—literally.

Elias pretended not to notice and went ahead with the wedding preparations.

But Zika, as all the Metaxa women, had a personality so strong, it would occasionally become extreme. And an extreme wedding it was! Elias's mother forbade her own in-laws, Corina's parents, to attend the wedding of their own daughter.

Elias and Corina went along with her wishes.

My godfather Takis accompanied the tearful bride to the church. Corina was such a beautiful bride, but so sad with tears running down her beautiful face.

A note on Takis, an amazing godfather and overall human being. More than simply accompanying my mother to the church for her wedding, he had already been an empathetic rock for her to lean on throughout her struggles. He was a father figure and friend to so many in my family—including myself.

When I was engaged to my now ex-husband and forever friend George, we at one point owned an athletic wear store together. Takis, a much older man in his eighties by then, made the great effort of taking a cab to the shop, from far away where he lived. A proud, kind man, Takis strode into our shop, looked George in the eye and said—"I want to meet the man who will marry my goddaughter." He then gave me a beautiful gift, a gold cross with my name engraved on the back—something I will treasure forever. Takis was there for me and before that, my mother Corina.

Corina's life route sculpted her character and her relationship with the Metaxas. She was only nineteen when she married my father, the product of a difficult childhood. She and her twin sister were just about one years old when their mother Olvia left their father Vassilis, only to return home when the girls were seventeen. This was in the 1940s when this kind of behavior was unthinkable.

Once again, similar repetitive life patterns and traits among generations. Mistakes copied subconsciously by characters that thought they were unique, but really, they were just repeating previous behaviors. Each individual vowing to be different and to leave his own mark only to unknowingly at the time copy paste personalities and life patterns.

This has gone on and on and families for generations, until someone in a new generation becomes aware of the patterns, and decides to change them for the better. Like how I am now attempting to bring a stop to the identical plot lines that have played out in my family for generations, by writing this book, by at least trying to create a clean slate for the next generations—my son, nieces, nephews, and their children.

We cannot change fate of course but we can learn and teach true love, self awareness, self knowledge and how to face turmoil with dignity. We must love, accept, cherish, and listen to our souls.

The Fruits of Strong Women

Despina

My great grandmother Despina, wife of Spyros Metaxa, was a unique woman in Greece. In the 1800's, surrounded by business*men*, she stepped forward and made her mark as an entrepreneurial female. She established and founded (with the assistance and blessing of Minister Miaoulis) "SA companies," a group of anonymous companies which still exist today.

Despina was an astute business woman, working daily alongside her husband, the founder of Metaxa, Spyros. Furthermore, she was a born philanthropist constantly providing free meals for the poor.

Everybody knew of her beautiful house in the city of Piraeus near the greatest Greek harbor. My great grandparents' home was built by the famous architect Chiller who had also built the palace of King George the first.

She was Despina of Piraeus to all the citizens of the town and even beyond. When she passed away, the entire town gathered for her funeral, genuinely mourning the loss and celebrating her remarkable life.

Zika

Despina would have loved my grandmother Zika had the two similar women ever met. My grandmother Zika was not a business woman in the way that Despina was, actually working in the company. However, her presence was felt in the factory every day, as she walked the halls of the Metaxa business offices and the factory floor, making it a point to know the name of every single employee in the company.

My grandma Zika visited the distilleries daily. In her "official" role within the company she organized the kitchen and the many company lunches in the famous dining room, as well as in the gardens. She was also in charge of the gardens, taking care of the beautiful orange trees, feeding the chicken, and the dogs, and carefully gathering the eggs the chicken had produced in a nice basket. She would then distribute the eggs to us and my uncle Spyros. We enjoyed fresh eggs every day. We also had a rooster and boy did my grandmother hate him! The feelings were mutual as he occasionally tried to attack her.

She often said that she would only be happy when she roasted the rooster and that's what she did one day presenting us for lunch one day a—"coq aux vin," a famous French recipe which translated to a rooster with a lot of wine. And that is how my grandmother's one time enemy, became a delicacy to be enjoyed by our family. Later in her life she also "roasted" a lot of my uncle Spyros' girlfriends as well as his wives (without the wine sauce)!

A Metaxa Family Portrait: Elias

Elias the Hunter

My father Elias grew up believing that his mother, my grandmother Zika, always preferred his brother Spyros to him due to the fact that Spyros almost died when he was a newborn and his mother believed that it was a miracle he lived. This made Elias stronger in all areas. It was this drive that made him excel in everything he did from producing amazing brandy to cooking unforgettable dishes for his friends and family.

But because of my grandmother's preference for Spyros, Elias constantly strived to prove how much better he was in all areas, unconsciously building a competitive relationship with his brother. (This also meant resenting his mother and blaming her for his failures starting at a young age.)

Throughout his life, he had many opportunities in the future to prove that he was a true Hercules, a Greek God who could do anything he put his mind on. Elias took advantage of each of these opportunities, even creating news ones where they did not exist.

His practical and analytical mind could build anything from a house to a distillery. He had vast technological knowledge and a problem solving mind.

As a young man he loved sports (mountain and water skiing among others). He was a fearless diver scuba diving deep down into the beautiful Greek seas and always returning with a vast collection of fish. Notably, over the years, Elias nearly reached the level of professional hunter, owning an impressive collection of guns which he handled with great skill and adeptness. His hunting expeditions took him all over Greece, the UK, Spain and Germany.

On a hunting trip with business associates in Germany, he met Emil Underberg, an agent for Underberg Liquors/ Digestive Drinks. Over the years Elias and Emil would become business partners as well as lifelong friends.

Emil lived in a beautiful house in Germany on a big property, ideal for hunting. One day they were hunting there and Elias became ecstatic when he shot a fancy rare humongous bird. It was a light moment when the bird fell flat on his back, just like in the comics!

But the light moment passed quickly when Emil ran to the scene screaming and cursing at Elias in German. The beautiful bird was one of his beloved pets! Apparently the "pets" had a bracelet on their foot and the hunters were not allowed to shoot them. Needless to say, that was a tense spot in the friendship.

From Hell to Hercules

Little Elias grew into a remarkably sensitive and resourceful human being. After he completed his studies in Dijon, he returned back home and rolled up his sleeves and plunged into work in the family business. He worked non stop at the warehouses, the offices—everywhere where there was work to be done. He drove all over Greece in a small van selling Metaxa. Later on he single handedly built the Metaxa Distilleries in Kifissia Greece where it still is today.

But the turning point in his life was when he met and fell in love with Corina. Theirs was one of the greatest love stories in our family tree. Elias has never ceased loving her from his very core, even now, 61 years later. Together Elias and Corina (Corelia to their friends) made a beautiful family, with three children and five grandchildren

Their love story waltzed through the decades, facing paradise and hell, uphills and downhills, making friends and enemies along the way. They persevered through kingdom to dictatorship to democracy and socialism in Greece. They cruised all over Greece and Italy in their sailing boat, Corelia entertaining numerous guests on it.

Meanwhile Elias never stopped working hard. He expanded his business mind in other areas. He founded a separate company which imported other liquors as well as chocolates and other sweets. He also got involved in the Greek Duty Free shops along with other partners. Last but not least he was president for many years of the Metaxa Anticancer Hospital, which was donated to Greece by his uncle.

Elias was a busy businessman, but through it all, a family man, always a devoted husband and father. He always found time to take his family skiing and traveling abroad as well as cruising around the Greek islands and mountains. He built a lovely house on Pelion, a beautiful Greek mountain where the family spent numerous summers and winters skiing and swimming.

When their children became adults and parents themselves, Elias gradually started slowing down, especially after the company was sold. Although he never stopped working. He would make brandy and liquors straight out of his personal barrels and give them to friends as a gift. One of these gifts was his beloved "Three Generations METAXA"—a simple minimal bottle with a handwritten number and signature on each bottle.

To this day Elias is still an expert cook and master blender, able to make anything imaginable that is edible or drinkable. He is an astute businessman and a person who enjoys nature and the good life.

PART III

Metaxa Stars

CHAPTER 7

Finding My Star

Boys and Girls, Men and Women

Boys, boys, boys . . .

This is not a song, it is the national anthem of Greece. Although women have achieved so much, worldwide and in Greece, in our country there is still an unspoken but loud behind the scenes competition between males and females.

It starts in the households but seeps into the workplaces and communities, continuing throughout the years. It shows up in not-so-subtle wording. About a successful lawyer or politician, who also happens to be female, it will be said—"For a woman she did exceptionally well!"

For a girl . . . For a woman . . .

When a woman is married in a Greek Christian Orthodox wedding ceremony, the priest reads passages instructing the woman to "obey and fear" the man. There is a common joke that if, when the priest speaks these exact words, the bride steps on the groom's foot, it means that she shall not obey but he must obey her! Even nowadays very few brides step on their husbands' toes.

Girls and later women constantly seek security and approval, which usually leads to wrong personal life choices. Boys and later men trying to prove their masculinity and born leadership qualities, to the other sex, their peers, and the whole world,

One does not need a degree in psychology to see the impact of these behavior and intergenerational patterns on relationships, marriages, children.

This cultural gender division has created in many Greek families a competition between brothers and sisters, first born and second born. It has created endless fights for approval, security, and unconditional love. Generations of siblings have grown up immersed in these beliefs, passing them along to their children, often while *believing* in their hearts that they are progressively minded. They believe they are breaking the chains of gender division while unconsciously living the beliefs instilled in them for their whole lives, reinforcing the chains instead.

Each and every generation striving to differentiate from the previous one and ending up forming identical patterns . . .

A Metaxa in a Non-Metaxa Home

The Metaxa Distilleries held and still hold a very special place in my heart. The childhood memories, the walks with my grandma in the gardens feeding the chickens and dogs, the family gatherings, and the famous dining room with the endless lunches.

On the business side of being a Metaxa, I remember the smells in the cellars, the busy production line, walking up and down the corridors, barging into my uncle's and father's offices, learning what my surname meant, the introduction to the business world, and my first business and public relations encounters that would later serve me as an adult working in the business. The admiration, passion and love for this unique product was instilled in me at an early age. Although I was a girl, I was a pretty determined Metaxa girl!

My brothers did not have a chance to work at the distilleries. When I was there they were younger and after school they immediately left Greece to study in the U.S.

Before the business was sold, I was in charge of the PR department. Among other tasks, I would take visitors on a guided tour around the distilleries talking to them about my family story and the making of Metaxa. My favorite highlight of the tour was in the cellars where I stood on a barrel and told our distillery guests about the ingredients in the few remaining sealed barrels from the 1800s with my ancestors' names etched on them—Spyros and Despina. One huge barrel for each of them has been kept safely and with extreme care, and still resides in the distillery to this day.

Then, in 1989 when Metaxa was sold to IDV a multinational beverages group who had a number of brands under their umbrella namely: J&B, Smirnoff, Gilbeys, Baileys, Malibu, and Archers, among others. At that point in my life I had just been accepted to a major university in Boston to earn my Masters Degree in marketing. But much to everyone's surprise, I decided to decline the offer to study in Boston, and study for a Masters in "real life" instead. Thus I was the only member of the Metaxa family who continued to work in the distilleries after the merge.

And work I did! What a bunch of surprises and shocks were in the basket for me—like little red riding hood when she met the big bad wolf. Working for a multinational company was the total opposite of working for the family business. There were no more lunches in the dining room, no more family fights and laughs, and no more familiar faces or relatives roaming the hallways. Automatic machines replaced the happy buzz of the production line. Our dining room became offices. No more dogs, chicken and eggs, or an angry rooster. No more grandma, papa, or uncle. The family business I had grown up in and loved so much, was now replaced with severe strict directors and aggressive on-the-rise managers and accountants.

My Name is . . . Boss. The New Boss.

Over my three years working for IDV (the multinational distribution company that bought Metaxa), I reported to three different managers.

The first one was extremely strict, demanding that I be in my office every morning at 7:30am. Work for everybody else started at 8:30. It was like having a big eye in the walls following my every move, always lurking around the next corner to catch me making a wrong move.

My second boss, however, was an exceptional human being and manager. He became my "mentor for life" and that's what I called him many years later, remaining friends with his wife and family for life.

The third general manager, the only Greek one incidentally, was equally strict. He was especially aggressive toward me, working me to all hours and expecting much more from me than the others.

When IDV took over and with the new range of Metaxa products, marketing was revamped from the beginning. Whereas before as a family we had one advertising agency for Metaxa, the multinational brought in a number of agencies to brief and distribute accordingly the numerous products under their umbrella.

We had an awesome Marketing Director with whom we spent endless hours simultaneously working and having fun. We were a great marketing team and I served on the team as brand manager for a number of products. This entailed a lot of traveling and late nights, checking the outlets, bars, restaurants, super markets, and long briefings and meetings with advertising agencies. Our days and nights were jam packed constantly promoting our products.

We were a close knit team and, similar to my relationship with my "mentor for life," all the brand managers became lifelong friends. We even had a marriage between a member of the marketing team and an auditor at the time!

It was a very demanding period for me but one I will always cherish. The lessons I learned accompanied me all my life.

Malibu

Since I was the only member of our family to cross over to IDV, as a joke people would ask whether I was included in the takeover price! The corporation's takeover brought a totally different approach to the business compared to when my father and uncle used to run it. But I still found a way to bring the feisty Metaxa spirit to my work.

As the multinational company had an umbrella of other products, I was brand manager for a few products, including Malibu. One of IDV's most well-known liquors, Malibu is forged in the consumer's mind as a tropical summer drink which is mainly true. However one of our aims was to deseasonalize Malibu. We had a superb plan which included a weeklong promotion trip at a Greek ski resort, during winter of course. It was a fancy winter sports resort a few hours from

Athens, surrounded by many bars and nightlife buzzing with electricity and energy.

During the days we served hot chocolate with Malibu (yummy!) at the ski lifts and at night we promoted the liquor at the resort bars. On one of those nights, a young woman at a bar was enjoying our Malibu shots perhaps TOO much! The shots apparently made her so hot that before we knew it, she was standing on the bars shedding her layers of winter clothing in a sensual strip tease. I remember the exact moment when our marketing director looked up and saw that the woman was totally naked standing on the bar over him. His eyes just about popped out of his head! Thinking fast, he hurried to cover her up—with a Malibu branded t-shirt we had on hand.

Baileys

Another product I handled as a brand manager was Baileys, the famous Irish liqueur. This entailed many trips to Ireland and a massive advertising campaign on TV as well as promotions in the bars.

One of my favorite bar promotions was more like a live version of a commercial. We hired a bunch of models who looked more like ordinary people having an after work drink at the bar. They sat at a prominent table in the middle of the bar, ordered a bottle of Baileys, and started drinking. As they drank, they intentionally got loud, laughing and dancing, and getting attention from the other customers. Soon, the waiters circulated through the bar, offering everyone free Baileys, saying it was comped by our models. When people asked the models why, they would say—"Because we love Baileys and are having such fun that we want to share it with you!" Worked like a charm—everyone in the bar would start waving down servers and ordering their own Baileys.

Hard Work

Smirnoff, Malibu, Baileys, Archers, and Gilbeys were some of the brands I handled—brands I learned to love as if they were my own. But behind the scenes, away from the funny stories, travel, late nights and fun of promoting the products, like any other business, there were hours of hard work back at the office. Meetings, brainstorming and business plans, budgets and making sure our products were properly distributed in the bars and restaurants.

As a true Metaxa I was not unaccustomed to hard work. Even back in the days when I was working at the family distilleries my life was more than strolling around and family lunches.

For instance every year I went with my uncle Spyros and other colleagues for a week to the Duty Free Food and Beverage Exhibition in Cannes. This was a very important meeting point where Metaxa had a booth among other international beverages, standing out as the only Greek spirit. This meant hours and hours on my feet, with a constant smile and high energy, offering people a taste of Metaxa, holding long discussions with strangers, exchanging cards and in the evening, long business meals in restaurants or hotels.

On other occasions I had to go to Malaga, Spain during major football matches where we had a Metaxa billboard in the court. I had to make sure that the billboard (which moved) was in its correct place, as well as spend hours setting it all up with the advertising agency we used for all the many athletic events where our billboards appeared.

Another one of those events that I enjoyed, was car racing, where we sponsored a car in the prototypes car racing for a whole year. Events like these gave me the chance to travel around the world making sure our sponsorship was running smoothly (literally speaking), while meeting interesting people and getting acquainted with the dangerous but fascinating car racing world.

A Dance of Work and Play

Many long hours of hard work were involved before and after the Metaxa-IDV merge. It was a constant dance of "work hard, play hard," a dance always powered by perseverance and resulting in lessons learned in experiences big and small alike.

It was learning bit by bit, step by step, through mistakes and falls.

It was having to occasionally trade my youthful spontaneity for aggressive behavior in a man's strong spirit (as in drink) world.

It was many degrees of alcohol in a bottle, many reflections in a glass.

It was high degrees, high performance.

It was flying high and falling down many times.

It was constantly facing the unasked question in the eyes of so many, "what the heck are you trying to prove?"

It was humor and irony, hope and disappointment, excitement and deceit, adrenaline and exhaustion.

It was high hopes, ambiguous results, joy and courage, relief and sustenance.

It was always, goals to be met, promises to be executed, all while simultaneously waltzing through my own personal life and turbulence.

We all go through the same more or less paths in our lives. People you know, friends or relatives, keep telling you to keep going on, to be strong. We all know this in theory but it takes inward drive which needs motivation.

No matter what one tells you, only when there is a sudden internal click, a reset mode that happens just like that—only then do you feel the meaning of perseverance.

It sometimes takes years of soul searching or practice, but once you get it you never let it go. It determines your life and your impact on your loved ones' lives.

I Did It My Way

The way of following your heart.

The way of enrolling in a marathon even if you just walk instead of run.

The way of going against all odds.

The way of speaking and acting your mind.

The way of living an unknown life with a well-known name.

The way of a billion compromises.

The way of numerous faults and many rewards.

The way of living life to its fullest.

The way of working for your family.

The way of carving your path outside of your family.

The way of being certain that your family is wrong yet following their exact same path in life.

The way of trying to prove your family wrong and end up proving them right.

★ ★ ★

CHAPTER 8

Relish or Repeat

Past, Present, Future

Why do we repeat patterns and mistakes, from the past generations, keeping them alive into the present and future ones?

Why do we repeat the mistakes that hurt us so much?

Why do we do exactly what was done to us?

Why do we follow the footsteps that lead us down the wrong paths?

Why does the tormented heart torment others?

We spend years of our lives stressing and worrying about relationships especially within the family.

We struggle,fight, cry, shout, separate, and reunite, over and over, in tear stained cycles.

We spend hours on couches, sometimes with friends, other times across from therapists, analyzing our relationships, reliving the past, trying to understand, trying to shut out the pain, and always vowing that next time it will be different.

We are so sure that we have all the answers, that we know right from wrong.

We make promises to ourselves and others that we are a different generation, one that has education, knowledge and experience the previous ones lacked, that we are positioned to make better choices than they did.

But we always follow the same identical patterns.

Many times we even phrase the exact same words. Hurtful words . . .

We are the next generation but we copy paste the previous ones.

If we cannot break out, how will the ones after us escape?

We read books, understand, nod in agreement and in anger about mistakes by the previous generation. And then we repeat those same mistakes.

We never want to hurt our loved ones like we were hurt, but we mostly do.

And just like the ones before, we are of course, unmistakable.

How will these patterns ever stop?

Who holds the key to a bright future for our children or grandchildren?

Only through unconditional love and understanding, maybe we will be able to turn the wheel and steer our individual boats the other way.

Relish or Repeat

We constantly repeat patterns and characteristics of the previous generation without even realizing it. This includes the small personality traits we inherit and mumble to ourselves in frustration, "God as I get older I am becoming just like my mother!" We repeat the traits we hate—sometimes, it seems, more than we model the traits we admire.

My mother for instance is obsessive about tidiness, constantly looking for something to clean, declutter, or clear away. She will pick up your plate to bring to the kitchen before you're done eating, remove your glass with one sip left in it, empty the ashtray while you are still enjoying your cigarette, fluff pillows on the sofa that are already over fluffed, and drop to her knees in an instant on all fours to pick up a loose thread on the floor. Her obsessive behavior used to irritate me to no end!

Guess what?

Unfortunately in the same way, I am now doing exactly the same and driving my son nuts!

Meanwhile, my mother sees herself as the most calm, stress free person in the world—a true zen master. But without realizing it she stresses about everything and spends hours over analyzing.

And because I've unconsciously followed in her footsteps, my middle name could be "stress" just like my mother's. Also just like my mother, I always think that I have conquered stress, that it is not affecting me. The truth is that stress conquered me in the form of an autoimmune disease that I am still managing every day.

Like my mother, I also believe that I am totally calm and zen when dealing with my teenage son and most of the time I even appear so. But our children sense our internal vibes just like we do the ones of our parents, and they, like us, unconsciously react in the same way. When my inner self is in chaos, it reflects in my outer self. Or in my son's words—"crazy!" So of course he also has a lot of stress which is manifested unfortunately in the same way, through health issues.

These personality traits go back for generations. These behavioral patterns trace a line through our family history, as is true in every family including yours.

My grandmother Zika was rejected by her in-laws and in her turn also rejected my mother Corina, who was also bitter about all her children's choice of life partners.

With my awareness raised about this pattern and a fierce determination to break it, I keep saying that I will respect and fully embrace my son's life partner—no matter what. Now that I have written this I sincerely hope that he will not come one day waving this book to me as evidence!

CHAPTER 9

5 Stars

The 5 stars on the METAXA 5 STAR bottle represent the 5 years that the product was in the barrel. The same applies for the 7 star bottle and the 12 star bottle.

Comparing my life to the product I love so much, created by the family members I love, over generations of ancestors—seems only natural.

Like how brandy matures over time in a barrel, I feel like I've been maturing in a barrel for my entire life. If I were to be a 5 star brandy, and if I were to recommend how YOU could be one too, here are 5 major attributes to develop in yourself.

#1: Be Original

Thousands of copies would follow, but there will always be only one original Metaxa.

Have we lost our originality as a species?

We live in a society where so many people and so much of what they do is fake. The few genuinely original people have worked for years, striving to to build and maintain their originality. This is no easy task in a fake world where people are so reluctant to be transparent and honest about who they really are.

How many relationships, friendships, and acquaintances are based on originality? Do we build and decorate our houses based solely on how we would like them to be or simply to impress the people who will be visiting?

What about our cars, our clothes, our possessions? There are the authentic few who act and dress based on their own clear personal identity, values, and preferences? But what about those who are living to be liked by others? Basing their lives on social media likes?

Likes like followers. How many lives have been turned into a daily game of instant gratification addiction, with insecure people around the planet craving "likes" from the moment they wake up in the morning until the moment they fall asleep at night? Liking their likes, following their followers, and going with the crowd, without stopping to give a thought to what they REALLY like or dislike, whom they REALLY want to follow—who they REALLY want to be, authentically.

How can we follow our hearts more?

This is one lesson I got from my original life—I learned to follow my heart, my real likes, to challenge my security and comfort zone, to fight for anything I truly believe in, to be and act genuinely at all times and in all situations.

My whole life has been guided by this inner force, one that makes me follow my heart and instincts in every moment. I immediately know, feel deep within, who I genuinely like and they become my lifelong friends. I can't fake likes!

Follow your heart. Be with the ones whom you love deeply and who love you right back just as deeply. Even when the odds are against you, like they were in my marriage and in the marriages of my mother and grandmother. Let your heart fly free and feel the force it gives you to fight for who and what you want in life. Love lets you ignore the obstacles, the nastiness, and plunge in. Love lights the torch that you can use to explore your life and make sure it is what you want it to be—and you are who YOU want to be in it!

Regret nothing. Live life at its fullest, and sip every beautiful moment just like you would sip and enjoy a Metaxa.

#2 Be Brave

After getting hit in the face with forceps as I was brought into this world, being brave was a choice mostly out of my control. It was be brave, or let life sweep me away and do what it wanted with me.

I braved visits to the eye doctors in Germany and all the surgeries from age three to fifteen.

I braved all the bullying from the other kids at school about my lazy crazy eye.

I braved being sent away to Switzerland by my parents at age 9 for a whole year, because I had asthma and the doctor said I had to live at a high altitude (which Greece is not). I went to a foreign school in a foreign land where I did not speak a word of French, the predominant language there. I slept and ate every day with strangers. I took phone calls from my parents in a tiny cubicle, always with a constant lump in my throat from holding back tears when hearing their voices.

Bravery or simply trying to survive under hard circumstances? Something everyone can relate to I believe.

But I did it. A year later, my asthma was cured, I had made new friends, and I spoke perfect French with a perfect accent.

I was brave because bravery was required. And I grew and became stronger as a result of it!

To be brave. To follow your heart. To close your eyes to anyone or anything that interferes with the path you choose to follow in life. That is the version of bravery that I wish for all of you reading this:

To have no regrets.

To learn from your mistakes .

To never underestimate the correct timing in life.

And to be aware of your actions and consequences.

They are of no more use to you. They make you sick. Detox!

#3: Be Innovative and Proactive

All of the stars in this chapter can apply to your personal life or your career, especially this one.

What is innovation? it's more than "a new method or idea" as stated in the dictionary. Innovation is the ability to act dynamically when life throws you challenges. It is being able to collect all those challenges like pebbles on the beach of life. Gather them in an imaginary bucket and sort them into two groups—toxic and treasures.

The toxic challenges are the ones that hold no value or lessons. You survived them and that is the end of the story. They are of no more use to you. Detox! Throw those pebbles as far into the ocean as you can. Each pebble that represents a toxic experience, situation, or person—throw it away. Make those pebbles unreachable.

Next, concentrate on the "goodies" in your bucket—the treasures. Take those pebbles out of your bucket, wash and polish each one, and put it somewhere safe.

These are the experiences that have taught you to solve problems proactively, to face life in an innovative way versus simply reacting to what is thrown at you. Your treasure pebbles are what you are made of and what you have become over the years.

Innovative and proactive is establishing a second business to supplement an already thriving family business. This is exactly what my father Elias did in the 1970's. Along with two good friends, he built the first DFS (Duty Free Shops) on the borders of Yugoslavia and Greece.

I followed his example and started working at sixteen years old, babysitting for nearby neighbors. Over the years I expanded my "babysitting business," sitting for the children of my university professors, also adding cooking and grocery shopping services to be even more valuable. Through it all, I practiced the budgeting skills I learned by watching my family working in Metaxa Distilleries. Years later, a classmate and I were talking about our childhood and she was still curious about why I always took the bus while everyone else hired cabs. I explained how hard I worked for my "pocket money" and didn't want to waste it on cab fare.

#4: Find The Fruit

Families always have ups and downs. Although sometimes it feels like there are more downs than ups.

When families are in business together, the downs can escalate from friendly competition into outright fights between parents, children, and siblings. What began as a simple case of sibling rivalry can become a court case of biblical proportions. Icy and painful silent treatments between parents and children can drag on for years.

Combine human nature with mistakes repeated generation after generation, sealed beliefs and stubborn attitudes, the clashing of egos and pride, and a mess of other abnormal psychology.

These dramatic stories have played out throughout history in family businesses of all sizes, all around the world. The stories will not stop but how each person in the story handles their role in it, can.

This is where we can accept the challenge to turn things around and end the most bitter and damaging outcomes that tear families apart, generation after generation—family businesses and perhaps even your own family story.

We can focus on the traits that hurt us, not to emphasize the pain but to learn from it and offer it as a tool for our children. We can use our painful family stories as a reminder to stop the unconscious cycle living in family reruns, decade after decade. We can break the chains with awareness and communication. We can be and do the opposite of what happened to us.

We can become stars in our family's future stories. We can lay the foundation so our §121§21§12§2§unconditional love, forgiveness, and acceptance. We can stand proudly and watch as they carve their own, unique, individual paths in the world. We can find the fruit in our family tree instead of getting tangled up in its painful vines.

But how can we practice this? As we all know theory stands miles away from practice.

I am no preacher or teacher. I have no diplomas in psychology other than the ones life handed me so generously. I have just been watching and thinking about how things repeat themselves in all families, both mine and yours, and want to put a full stop to the bad intergenerational patterns here and now.

It is not enough to just do the opposite of what the previous generations did, because those actions might also lead to disastrous results.

For example, the previous generation of Metaxas ahead of me was diligent in their parenting—almost to a fault. You see, they came from a generation where parents suffocated their children with love and an abundance of attention. This method was based on a popular saying in Greece during those times that too much love never hurt anybody. Their parents suffocated them, so our parents followed in their footsteps and did the same to us. And when I say suffocated with love, I mean all the things that come with that including control and hovering over their children's shoulders, giving opinions on all their decisions, and dictating the course of their lives. All in the name of love!

What was the result? Revolutionary acts from us children—now adults. We became so wary of too much love, too much attention, even when it was positive, that many of us had trouble with commitment. We tended to run away from anyone that showed us "too much love."

These traits, these phobias and misunderstandings about what true love really was, in essence sealed our fates, charting courses for our personal relationships. We became stingy with love and affection, afraid of "spoiling" our children.

This pattern, repeated over and over, ultimately created insecure adults who showered their children with the love they felt that they had missed out on.

And the life chain goes on and on.

This is where I have decided to stop it, partly through exposing these patterns in this book the way I have, through my family stories. Not just to end the patterns in my own family, but as a way of helping you spot similar toxic patterns in your family tree, so you can throw away the bad fruit, prune the dead branches, and find the goodies that remain—the things you DO want to pass on to the next generation!

Your wisdom and maturity will be the keys to doing this. Intelligence obtained from life not from a college degree, but from self awareness and the willingness to draw a line in the sand.

This is where you take the goodies and seal them with boundaries. This is where you start writing your own unique life story, untainted by the past.

#5: Declutter Your Mind

I always thought I was a real extrovert. This is based on the fact that, as a child, I would talk a lot. My family nicknamed me "the chatterbox."

Well guess what? I was really the clutter box not the chatterbox. As casual, mostly meaningless words poured from my mouth, I kept all the clutter swirling around in my mind, my REAL thoughts—in a secret box.

I didn't talk about the things that hurt me, bugged me, or made me anxious. I didn't reveal my most serious, important thoughts.

My chatter existed purely on the surface of life.

Unknown to me then, I was doing exactly what I was taught as a young girl: Keeping to myself, not sharing my feelings, never expressing my anger, and all the while letting it boil and take root deep down inside me. I tucked away into my emotional clutter box, all those feelings, emotions, anger, and pain.

Unfortunately, all those things eventually escaped into my body.

When I became aware of this a few years ago, I started intentionally opening the box, trying to declutter my heart, body, mind, and soul. In the process, I was horrified to learn that I was encouraging the same habits in my son. Without even realizing it, I had encouraged him to create his OWN clutter box for his emotions, feelings, and thoughts!

Here I was, thinking I was chatting, really talking to him, but once again, maybe from a lifetime of practice, I was sealing the "real" things inside. I was parading through life with a mask on my face.

Does any of this ring a bell for you? What's in your clutter box?

I am grateful that I have finally torn the mask and am now breathing fresh air. I am learning and teaching by example, true communication, facing my emotions instead of turning my back to them.

Boxed up emotions become traumatic. Acknowledge the contents of your clutter box, accept that they exist, and then RESET.

Once we reset our lives, hopefully our children's lives will follow our example.

A METAXA FAMILY PORTRAIT

My Grandmother Zika

In accordance with Greek tradition, I was named after my father's mother Zika. Here is the story of my namesake, and in my eyes, "the original" Zika Metaxa.

My dearly beloved grandmother Zika was born in1906 to a middle class family. When she met my grandfather Andreas (after whom my brother was duly named) she was a stunning young girl with green eyes, ebony black hair, and velvet skin. She was tall and graceful, a portrait of class in every way, and that is how she remained until she died at age 94. No wonder my grandfather Andreas fell madly in love with her as soon as he set eyes on her! He almost immediately asked her to marry him.

But this spontaneous act cost him, because in those days you needed family approval in order to marry. My great grandparents were not alive at the time, but my grandfather had two brothers, both unmarried, and both with a big say in all family matters.

When they found out months later that Andreas was married, they were furious. Furthermore my grandmother

Zika, in their eyes, was a poor girl, not good enough for their brother. They ordered my grandfather to divorce her, threatening to disinherit him and throw him out of the Metaxa business (in which he was already working and was already growing quickly).

When my grandmother Zika learned of all this, she immediately left her husband with no discussion at all. She disappeared because she loved him dearly and did not want to be an obstacle in his career or a problem in his life. But what nobody knew at the time, including Zika herself, was that she was pregnant!

She found refuge in a relative's house in a village and had a miscarriage so severe that it almost cost Zika her life. One of the relatives took pity on the poor young girl and found a way to get word to my grandfather Andreas about what had happened.

Andreas, in great despair, told his brothers. Both brothers had second thoughts about their original judgment of my grandmother, and felt guilty, realizing that Zika was a very dignified young woman who truly loved their brother. Genuinely wanting to make up for all the pain they caused, they did everything possible to find her and bring her back, begging her forgiveness. My grandparents were remarried after that, and were never separated again until death did they part.

But my grandmother Zika was severely traumatized psychologically and physically after the ordeal. Even more so when almost a year later she was informed by doctors that she would never conceive again.

Night after night she shed tears of despair, anger, bitterness, and fear for the future. Andreas, in agony, watched his beautiful wife get thinner and thinner and walk through life with a haunted look in her beautiful green eyes.

Once more he turned to his brothers for help. Now united, they found a specialized therapeutic clinic (we would call it a "spa" nowadays) in Switzerland. They immediately took my grandmother there and settled her into her room where specialist doctors invested round the clock care in her physical and mental health, including a favorite, daily therapeutic mud baths! Gradually the color came back to her beautiful face and the weight that she had lost, returned. And with those things, another special gift—the seed of a new Metaxa! A true miracle, my grandmother was now pregnant with what would become her first child, my uncle Spyros. A Metaxa boy was on the way, a time for joy and celebration as we know from Greek tradition!

But destiny had not yet finished its power games with Zika . . .

Spyros was born with a birth defect, a severe problem in his tiny stomach which, if not operated on immediately, could kill him. With such precarious surgery on a newborn, especially in those days, the doctor made no promises other than that they would do their best to save little Spyros.

Zika's newborn son was just two days old when he went into emergency surgery. She and Andreas had no other options. Through tears, my grandmother handed over tiny Spyros on a pillow to the doctors—and then collapsed.

She then found a little church in the hospital gardens, fell to her knees, and began praying to the Virgin Mary. She prayed for a miracle that would save her newborn's life. She begged not to be derived of motherhood abruptly and against her will yet again. Zika was a young girl who simply dreamed of having a family—that's all she ever asked for. It was something so simple and natural to others but seemed so unattainable to her.

My grandmother spent the entire 20 hours of the surgery on her knees, praying in that garden.

Her prayers reached the Virgin Mary, and Spyros was saved. This was a true miracle especially then, in 1935, given the severity of the birth defect and technology available to correct it.

Spyros was given back to his mother on his little pillow with infinite stitches from his belly to his chest. These stitches over the years took the form of a sword—Spyros' own, personal sword that would accompany him for all his life.

★ ★ ★

CONCLUSION

Modeling Positivity

I am no preacher or guru. But through working on myself extensively over the last few years, I now see many aspects of my life, through new eyes.

For many years I carried a lot of anger. Rather than expressing that anger, I bottle it up like poison deep within me. I believe that eventually that poison triggered an autoimmune disorder in me—a sharp awakening to the power of repressed emotions!

Fortunately, therapy, alternative mind and body health techniques, and coaching, had an immense positive effect on my life. I learned how to understand, forgive, and move on. I learned how we almost always repeat our parents' behaviors, even, and maybe especially, the traits we dislike the most.

This is where we realize that the fighting is useless. It is like going to battle with the image of yourself in a full length mirror. There will be no winners and only losers. I learned that the secret is to create some distance from our emotions and observe the truth as it is, rather than how we "wish" it was. With distance, we can finally accept the good with the bad, and learn from both. We need to accept what we cannot change and take our time to live every day to its fullest, such a cliche but so true. I am still working on this one!

Thanks to this extensive and deep work on myself, I was finally able to proceed with my life in a new and mature way.

And then, on top of all that, something unexpected happened. I noticed that when we change our perspectives, others around us follow our lead and do the same! When we focus on the good, that is what we will bring into our lives and that is what we will model for our children and loved ones. That will transform us from victims into role models.

Perseverance, His Name is Angelos

Speaking of role models, the one I am about to pay tribute to, is the picture of perseverance. He is my brother Angelos.

Angelos, my "Angy," has faced an unprecedented storm of challenges in his life. At one point, those challenges culminated into a figurative war engulfing him, surrounding him by dragons raining venom and fire down on him, trying to demolish him. To offer another maybe more relatable visual, imagine taking a walk through nature on a sunny peaceful day, minding your own business, and suddenly you are attacked by strangers hurling rocks at you for no reason. You have nowhere to hide. That was the equivalent of the challenges my brother was forced to face for many years.

Because of his strength in facing these challenges head on and persevering to their peaceful conclusions, my Angy will always be a role model for myself and our family. He went through hell and back, fell down over and over, but managed to stand up every time. Not only did he stand, but he then climbed mountains, literally (as one of his hobbies) and figuratively.

He climbed mountains, swam in a turbulent ocean full of nasty, greedy sharks, and walked through miles and miles of landmines, until he overcame all of his problems and reached the other side—the sunny side. And throughout it all, Angelos remained positive and determined that it would eventually work out. Patience, when paired with perseverance, can be a life preserver.

Only he in his heart knew how difficult it actually was to persevere in the face of his challenges. Just like only I fully understand my own difficulties in life, and only you understand yours. That is where empathy for others comes into the picture. I can encourage all of you to "persevere!!!"—but only you know what it will take and how long it will take. In theory it is easy advice to give, but sometimes when it comes to our everyday challenges the last thing we want to do is listen to the advice of others. We don't always want to take care of ourselves, to meditate, do yoga or other activities that keep us centered while in the middle of storms. We often forget to breathe. It seems easier to overindulge in food, alcohol, or other substances that help us escape from the stress of life. I know, I've been there. The Bridget Jones' Diary movies are among my favorites because of their take on empathy.

Maybe it would be easier if we learn to stop and count our blessings. Maybe if we learn to pause and find a way to be there for the ones we cherish. Maybe doing these things can help us not necessarily overcome, but get through our problems and face tomorrow with a different attitude. Maybe, in the spirit of Angy, we can use positivity, perseverance, and patience to slay our dragons and climb the mountains to a better day!

★ ★ ★

EPILOGUE

3 Generations

My father Elias, now age 85, is a man with many passions and interests—fishing and sailing today, and when he was a younger man—scuba diving, car racing, and building houses and factories. But his one big passion today, second only to my mother Corina, is creating and producing spirits, especially brandy.

He was the Master Blender for Metaxa Distilleries from 1960 to 1989. He never stopped blending even after the company was sold. He created many more spirits such as the Coutsikos liqueurs, brandy and ouzo, as well as a brand new factory from scratch for those Coutsikos products. This factor still exists and is situated in the town of Volos, a three hour drive from Athens.

But the one trait that sustained my father Elias throughout his life and through all the difficulties he faced, was and still is, his perseverance. This trait also helped him to perfect his hobbies. It is in true perfection that he recently created an eternal brandy, proving that age is irrelevant when you follow your passions and dreams. This is the story of how that eternal brandy came to be.

For all these years he had kept some of the original brandy inherited from his father Andreas, but manufactured during the years 1920-1923 by his grandfather Spyros, in his own private cellars in oak barrels. Using all his senses and this reserve he created an exquisite brandy which at the time (a few years ago) he bottled in simple bottles and gave as a gift to his friends. But anyone who tasted it wanted more and kept raving about it.

In 2020 he decided to unveil this unique product to the world instead of keeping it for private use. He contacted the House of Metaxa (Metaxa Distilleries) currently owned by Remy Martin.

In collaboration with them and working closely with their Master Blender, my father created the most exquisite Metaxa EVER! It is a real jewel, his last and most perfect personal creation. And as such it is bottled in an exquisite carafe housed in a unique and luxurious box.

Elias named his jewel—AEN THREE GENERATIONS.

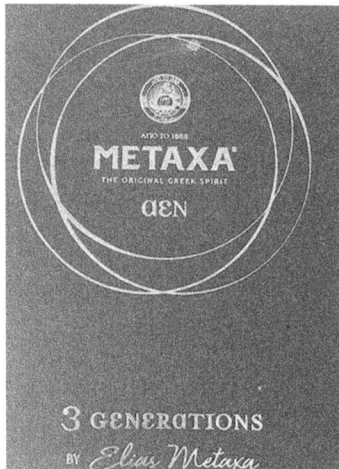

AEN Packaging

AEN in Ancient Greek means "eternal" and fittingly, the beautiful logo consists of three rings, representing the three generations of the family, as my father is the third generation. They also symbolize the trinity of Legacy, Terroir, and Craftsmanship. The decanter is not there to just hold the spirit. It is part of the experience, to feel the weight of the crystal and then to pour the liquid.

The Custom Designed AEN Decanter

In March of 2022, after a series of pandemic-related delays, my father and the House Of Metaxa FINALLY, officially launched AEN!

The unforgettable evening was held in the cellars of Metaxa Distilleries, the very cellars my father built from scratch, the same ones I used to cruise as a kid with my grandma.

A full life cycle.

Our family was there as well as the international and Greek Press. I will forever hold in my heart the image of my father making his speech with images of his ancestors behind him on a video wall. I will forever remember the goosebumps that tingled on the surfaces of my arms when he pronounced the signature statements of his speech:

AEN 3 GENERATIONS
is the flagship of the House of Metaxa.

AEN 3 GENERATIONS
is the diamond of the House of Metaxa.

It is the epitome of my craftsmanship and
the closing of the life cycle for me.

I will forever hold his happy smile and eyes—to quote my friend Maria—"when a person laughs wholeheartedly his eyes laugh too."

Three generations is my father's first and last dream. His own unique legacy.

Craft.

Harmony.

Perseverance.

Eternity.

YA SU! (To your health.)

THE END

www.ingramcontent.com/pod-product-compliance
Lightning Source LLC
Chambersburg PA
CBHW030959090426
42737CB00007B/608